Original title:
The Call of the Whale's Song

Copyright © 2025 Creative Arts Management OÜ
All rights reserved.

Author: Jasper Montgomery
ISBN HARDBACK: 978-1-80587-424-9
ISBN PAPERBACK: 978-1-80587-894-0

Gala in the Gentle Currents

In the sea, the fish all dance,
With fins and tails, they prance.
A whale suggests, "Let's have a ball!"
But who will lead? It's hard, after all.

The squids wear ties, the crabs bring snacks,
As seaweed confetti flows like wax.
A dolphin jokes, "Where's all the wine?"
The shrimp reply, "It's brine, not fine!"

The turtles shuffle, slow and wide,
While jellyfish wave with strange pride.
A seahorse spins in dazzling flair,
Until a big wave sends him in the air!

They all laugh as they land with a splash,
With bubble noises, they make a crash.
In currents kind, they find their bliss,
In salty fun, they seal the kiss!

Euphonic Waves Embrace

A baritone hum flows through the blue,
As fish decide what's best to do.
With synchronized moves, they'll form a crew,
Imitating a flair while dancing adieu.

A crab takes the stage with a mic in claw,
"Who's ready for a stunning jaw?"
The crowd erupts, "Give us more!"
As underwater sounds begin to roar!

The seagulls watch with disbelief,
As a clownfish starts the comic relief.
"Why did the oyster refuse the dance?"
"Because he was shy, caught in a trance!"

With every beat, the ocean sways,
As sea creatures toast to goofy days.
In harmony, they sway and groove,
With laughter echoing, they can't improve!

Rhythmic Murmurs Underneath

In the deep, a tune so bright,
A fishy dance, a silly sight.
Grouper groovy with a grin,
Bubble parties, let's begin!

Octopuses shake it too,
With eight limbs, they form a crew.
The water sways, the kelp does sway,
Under the waves, they laugh and play.

Chants of the Ocean Floor

Coral choirs sing off-key,
As starfish twirl in harmony.
A crab tap dances with delight,
While sea cucumbers take flight.

Anemones sway with joy,
Tickled by the waves, oh boy!
Each one tries to find their part,
In this silly ocean heart.

Trill of the Tides

Seagulls join in with a squawk,
Cracking jokes 'till snails can walk.
The tide rolls in with laughter loud,
A wobbly whale joins the crowd.

Bubbling sounds of fishy fun,
Pinch a shrimp, make sure to run!
A blend of giggles fills the brine,
As mermaids sip their salt-filled wine.

Beneath the Echoing Waves

From the depths, a gurgle flows,
Crabs wear hats, but who really knows?
Jellyfish float with graceful flair,
Throwing a party without a care.

The flatfish sport a sly disguise,
Pretending not to see the skies.
With bubbles raised, the sea does hum,
In this wacky world, oh here we come!

Marine Melodies in Distant Waters

Bubbles rise with a cheesy tune,
Fish gather round, saying, "What a boon!"
Dolphins dance, with fins in fine flair,
Crabs pinch along, with nibbles to share.

Octopus joins with eight-armed grace,
Tickling shells in a jellyfish race.
Turtles tap to the beat of the tide,
As sea stars groove, their arms open wide.

Aetherial Cadence

Up in the blue, where echoes abound,
A curious squid makes a wiggly sound.
Whales blow bubbles, chilled by their song,
But fish just giggle, "This can't be wrong!"

Crabs with top hats, a quirky parade,
Tap dance on reefs made of glittering jade.
Seahorses twirl with a swish and swirl,
In this ocean ball, life whirls like a pearl.

The Ocean's Heartbeat

The sardines drum, in a shimmering line,
Grouper grins wide, feels simply divine.
A whale's grand solo, a bellow so bold,
Cracks up the mackerel, a sight to behold.

Pufferfish puff, trying to exceed,
But a clownfish bubbles, "Just take heed!"
A sea turtle chuckles at all of the fuss,
Saying, "Relax, it's just us!"

Symphonies of Surf and Swell

In the surf's embrace, a melody glides,
Seashells clap hands, a whimsical ride.
Starfish chime in with a twinkly pop,
While otters tumble, they'll never stop!

With seaweed strings, a band comes alive,
Playing the hits of their watery jive.
Frogs croak rhythm, and gulls take flight,
Under the waves, laughter takes the night.

Verses in the Tidal Flow

In the ocean blue, a whale did hum,
Its tunes so loud, they made fish run.
With every note, a splash and a spray,
The dolphins danced, hip-hip-hooray!

The octopus joined with a funky beat,
Tapping its tentacles, oh so neat.
While seagulls laughed, they flapped their wings,
Who knew the sea had such funny things?

Reflections in the Sapphire Waters

Beneath the waves, the seaweed sways,
Echoing laughter in curious ways.
A whale's big voice tickles the tide,
Making sardines giggle and glide.

A chorus of bubbles flew up like jokes,
Even the crabs gave silly pokes.
As the wave rolls in, the shouts are clear,
Who knew the ocean could spread such cheer?

Lyrical Surge of the Sea

Across the surf, a symphony plays,
Whale tunes reverberate, here to stay.
Fish do a jig, while turtles sway,
In this underwater cabaret.

The seahorse twirled with quite the flair,
Knock-knock jokes floated in the air.
The sea cucumbers tried to keep pace,
But ended up rolling all over the place!

The Ocean's Timeless Chorus

In the depths below, a humor parade,
Whales cracking jokes in the ocean's shade.
"Why did the fish blush?" they did sing,
"Because it saw the ocean's bling!"

As bubbles burst with each funny quip,
Even the starfish joined in a flip.
A whale's great laugh, echoing wide,
Made all the sea creatures swell with pride!

Resonance of the Sea Giants

Bubbles burst in laughter, oh so bright,
Fins flap like comets, taking flight.
The kraken winks, with a cheeky grin,
As fish in tuxedos dance and spin.

With seaweed wigs, the party's alive,
Turtles tap dance, oh how they jive!
Jellyfish glow like disco lights,
While dolphins throw in wild water fights.

The Song of Ancient Waters

A whale with a megaphone sings out loud,
Ruffling the feathers of a nearby crowd.
Octopus DJs, spinning tunes with flair,
While seals do the conga, without a care.

Deep down below, there's a clam in a hat,
Swaying to rhythms, imagine that!
Crabs join in, clapping claws with glee,
It's the wildest party under the sea.

Chorus of the Coral Isles

Starfish sit back, sipping on sea brew,
Sardines serenade with a jazzy hue.
The parrotfish squawk, trying to compete,
Making up verses with a swishy beat.

In the sandy lounge, a pelican prances,
Every flap of the wings leads to more dances.
The seahorse roars like a rockstar on stage,
While eels play the bass, full of rage.

Heartstrings of the Horizon

Walruses waltz, cheeks puffed out wide,
With a flippered flair, they take each stride.
The horizon chuckles at their blushing delight,
As the sun sets, painting the night.

With sea cucumbers sporting trendy shades,
Caught in the moment, nobody fades.
Jellybeans tumble in a foamy parade,
While the ocean hums softly, serenely played.

Ocean Echoes

In the deep blue, fish dance around,
A beluga's giggle, a quirky sound.
Sharks wear bow ties, octopuses play,
Seaweed sways gently, in a quirky ballet.

Dolphins do flips, such comic display,
Pufferfish puff, then float away.
Crabs wear their hats, as they scuttle and scheme,
Every splash brings joy, in this ocean dream.

Melodies Beneath the Waves

Bubbles burst forth, like laughter in tide,
Eels sing a tune, with their heads held wide.
Starfish clap hands, in a coral bar,
Whales hum soft tunes, from near and far.

Clownfish joke, with faces so bright,
The sea's got a rhythm, pure delight.
Jellyfish glow, like disco lights,
Underwater parties, every day and night.

The Siren's Serenade

Siren's voice echoes, with a giggly twist,
Mermaids sing songs, with a bubbly gist.
Their tails flop and flounder, in a droll way,
While fish join in, having fun in the bay.

Oh, the sea turtles bob, with a giggling flair,
As seagulls join in, without a care.
They dance in circles, making quite the scene,
In this aquatic world, where laughter's supreme.

Whispers of the Deep

Turtles whisper secrets, from mullet to ray,
The sea's full of tales, in a comical sway.
Anemones tease, with their tickling arms,
While a big whale winks, with its charming balms.

Squids draw with ink, in a splashy affair,
Creating art portraits, with joking flair.
The ocean chuckles, with waves that tease,
Life's a big joke, in the salty breeze.

Odes to the Sirens

In the ocean's grand café, they sing,
Bubbles up and laughter takes wing.
With each note, they throw a splash,
Fish come dancing, making a dash.

They tease the sea with playful jest,
Even dolphins pause—who's the best?
With a wink and a flip, they chime,
A chorus that flows like sweet lime.

Seagulls drop in for an encore show,
Crab loungers clap—oh, what a throw!
The only rule is to giggle and sway,
For in this deep, it's a funny ballet.

The Rhythm of the Deep

Underneath the waves, they groove,
Tails swaying, making a move.
With guffaws so loud, they echo around,
Even the octopus joins in with sound.

Shells clap together, beat keeps strong,
While the fish form a line, dancing along.
To the rhythm of splashes and giggles so sweet,
The whole ocean buzzes to their funky beat.

A crab DJ spins, with a flip of a claw,
While turtles slow dance, just a little in awe.
The deep is alive with chuckles galore,
As laughter bounces from shore to shore.

Ballet of the Whales

In velvet blue, they pirouette,
Majestic tails, a sight that's set.
With each dip and rise, a splashy show,
Oh, how they twirl, high and low.

They twine and twist in a playful spree,
Manta rays join, what glee we see!
With a twinkling starfish leading the pack,
Their laughter echoes as they swirl and crack.

A grand finale with bubbles tossed,
The art of the sea, never lost.
For in this ballet, joy takes the stage,
The ocean's laughter breaks every cage.

Unheard Crescendo

Beneath the waves, a giggle grows,
A symphony of gurgles, who knows?
With a tickle and splash, they play along,
In the unspoken, they sing their song.

Turtles chuckle, the fish do flip,
In the rhythm of ripples, they take a trip.
Invisible notes fill the wet expanse,
As eels do boogie, lost in their dance.

The underwater world whispers and hums,
Full of humor, without the drums.
For in this deep, where silence seems,
Live the echoes of laughter and dreams.

The Ocean's Soulful Choir

In the blue, the fish do sway,
As they gather for a play.
Bubbles popping, laughter rings,
While the starfish tap and sing.

A seal jokes with a laughing gull,
Sharing tales of tides and mull.
Octopus with tentacles grand,
Plays the drums with a clever hand.

Dolphins dance with acrobatic flair,
Squid just wiggle, but don't care.
Harmony in salty waves,
While the crab misbehaves.

A whale blows a note so low,
Fish giggle with the ebb and flow.
In this choir, all is bright,
Under water, joy takes flight.

Veils of Sound Underwater

In the depths, a melody starts,
Fish are busting out the arts.
Clams are clapping with their shells,
Echoing like little bells.

Jellyfish sway like graceful lace,
While turtles trot with silly pace.
Grouper grins and joins the fun,
As sea urchins roll, one by one.

A pufferfish tries to sing out clear,
But puffs up in a fit of cheer.
And anglerfish lights up the scene,
Like a disco ball, all agleam.

Echoes rise like bubbles in air,
All are jamming without a care.
In ocean's embrace, laughter flows,
As the sound of friendship grows.

Murmurs from the Sonic Depths

Whispers swirl in currents deep,
As fishy secrets waddle and creep.
A whale's giggle reverberates round,
Tickling seaweed without a sound.

Nudibranchs dance with colors bright,
While crabs juggle throughout the night.
Blowfish puff with a comedic flair,
As sea cucumbers stop and stare.

In rock caverns, echoes bounce,
With playful banter, fish announce.
Barnacles beg for a spotlight,
As bubbles burst with sheer delight.

Yet all's serene in the aquamarine,
With not a care, just simple glee.
From sonic depths, mischief flows,
And the ocean's humor surely grows.

Dance of the Deep Sea Baritone

Down where the sunlight starts to fade,
A baritone croons, serenades.
With a belly flop, he makes a splash,
While the shrimp cheer and do the bash.

Angels of the sea light up with joy,
As clownfish play and deploy.
In a conga line, the sea sponges sway,
To the rhythm of laughter, come what may.

The sea turtle spins, looking quite bold,
With a swish of his fins, he breaks the mold.
The lobster joins with a step and twirl,
As the reef bustles, the colors swirl.

A whale's deep laugh undulates far,
Guiding the dance beneath the star.
In ocean's theater, joy imparts,
With every beat, the sea has hearts.

Songs Carried by Current

Bubbles rise with a giggle,
Fish dance in a silly jig.
A dolphin sneezes, quite a riddle,
While squids juggle, oh so big.

Turtles tap their flippers loud,
Seahorses dress for a rave.
Crabs break out to form a crowd,
With all the moves they crave.

Whales hum in a playful way,
Making waves with goofy grins.
Even the octopus wants to sway,
Shaking limbs as the dance begins.

In this frothy underwater,
Life's a laugh beneath the waves.
So join the fun and be a starter,
The ocean's song the current braves.

Sorrowful Serenade of the Sea

Once a fish wore a frown,
A clam sighed, 'What a day!'
With coral dressed in a gown,
They sang of love far away.

A crab lost his favorite shell,
Jellyfish floated, feeling blue.
They whispered tales with a swell,
Of the happy times they knew.

A whale scratched his head with woe,
'Why must the sea be so strange?'
Yet bubbles formed in a row,
Bringing laughter in exchange.

Through sorrow, joy still swam,
The ocean holds both sweet and sad.
With giggles, sighs, they cram,
And make the deep less bad.

Mysteries of the Deep Blue

Underneath where shadows creep,
A goldfish dreams of a crown.
Questions asked by creatures deep,
As mysteries swirl all around.

A puzzled squid sketched a map,
While stingrays rolled with delight.
What lies beyond this sea gap?
Could it be a sea serpent's sight?

An old turtle shared a laugh,
Tales of treasure, real or fake.
The secrets of the ocean's path,
For every giggle, a heartache.

Down where the sun is shy,
Life's a riddle wrapped in foam.
In the dark, laughter will fly,
For in the depths, all roam.

Whales' Serenade at Dusk

As day fades into twilight glow,
Whales gather for their evening show.
With deep notes that echo and sway,
They croon of fish that got away.

One playful whale stretched so grand,
Drew in bubbles with a wave of his hand.
'Tell me, do you think they care,
When we sing and dance with flair?'

As the stars blink and sparkle bright,
Waves chuckle at the silly sight.
With songs of joy that pierce the night,
They'd laugh till dawn, a pure delight.

Under the moon, they share the fun,
Whales know how to lighten the ton.
In their hearts, the ocean's beat,
Each serenade feels so sweet.

Rhythms of the Deep Blue

In ocean's depths, a giggle plays,
A fishy tune that brightens days.
With every splash, a joke unfolds,
In salty waters, laughter molds.

The turtles dance with silly moves,
Playing tag in playful grooves.
While dolphins spin in joyous glee,
Their underwater jubilee!

A crab does tap, a shrimp does prance,
Beneath the waves, they start to dance.
The seaweed sways, the sun's a tease,
As laughter floats in ocean breezes.

Oh, how the bubbles rise and pop,
In deep blue, where fun won't stop.
A chorus of mirth beneath the swell,
In watery realms where joy does dwell.

The Soundscape of Giants

In the sea, the whispers roam,
Big fellows jive, they call it home.
With booming laughs that shake the deep,
The tales they tell may make one weep.

They gather round for wacky rhymes,
Their voices echo, bending times.
A beluga chuckles, 'What a show!'
While fishy friends all line up, aglow.

A grumpy grouper joins the fray,
Complaining, 'Why swim every day?'
But then he bursts in laughter bright,
For in the depths, it feels so right.

From crusty rocks to sandy floors,
The giants share their funny scores.
As songs of joy fill up the tide,
With each new wave, more jokes collide.

Enchanted Waters' Melody

Whimsical waves in dances sway,
As silly fish come out to play.
With giggles echoed through the sea,
They sing of life and revelry.

A fish in specs reads poetry,
With puns of 'scale' and 'sea-crets' free.
And all the shells chime in with cheer,
As ocean mates draw ever near.

Beneath the gales, a mermaid sighs,
With laughter sparkling in her eyes.
She juggles sea cucumbers with grace,
Making the fishy crowd embrace.

As waves crash down and tide rolls high,
The music flows and spirits fly.
In enchanted depths, where jokes do gleam,
They dance through currents, all a dream.

Songs Carried by Currents

Bubbles rise with gleeing tunes,
Echoing joy beneath the moons.
Flipping flounders, cheeky squids,
Singing tales of clumsy bids.

A starfish who thinks he can boogie,
Challenging crabs to a dance so groovy.
While octopus dons a silly hat,
Declaring, 'I'm the one—what do you think of that?'

With currents swirling, laughter flies,
As seaweed sways beneath the skies.
A concert where the fish unite,
In percussion of shells, what a sight!

From reef to deep, the fun is cast,
With every wave, the giggles last.
So grab your fins, let's make a scene,
In waters where we're endlessly keen!

Sonorous Myths from the Deep

In the depths, a fish so grand,
It sings of seas and drifting sand.
Its voice, a burr, a joyful croon,
Makes turtles dance to quite the tune.

Octopus grooves with all its might,
Seahorses twirl in pure delight.
A kraken's laugh bubbles up free,
Tickling waves with a jellyfish spree.

The whale's got jokes, oh what a sight,
Making dolphins snicker with pure delight.
Each splash a punchline, each dive a jest,
In the ocean jest, it's truly the best!

So let us plunge in this watery glee,
Where laughter and echoes swim wild and free!
The depths aren't just serious, oh who knew?
They're filled with jokes and a giggling crew!

Echoing the Infinity Below

Down below, where sparkles reside,
A narwhal hums, oh what a ride!
With a horn like a pencil, it takes a chance,
Creating bubbles that jiggle and dance.

A clam tells tales with a wink, so sly,
As fishes giggle while swimming nearby.
The deep-sea disco's quite a blast,
With starfish spinning, no moment a past.

Crabs in tuxedos sway with flair,
While eels in tuxes give quite a scare.
Each coral reef echoes with cheer,
As the funny fish swim and persevere.

Oh hear the laughter, the fishy delight,
In the ocean's waves, everything feels right.
Where every murmur's an inside joke,
And laughter's the language of the ocean folk!

Rhapsody of the Hybrid Ocean

In the hybrid depths, where puns collide,
Lurks a fish that's half-guest, half-guide.
With a goggle-eyed stare and a cheeky grin,
It sings silly songs of where to begin.

The dolphins flip, with laughter they roll,
While anglerfish glow, taking on a role.
Their disco lights sparkling, a vibrant show,
Where every fin move steals the spotlight's glow.

Squids with mustaches, oh what a sight,
Swirl in the currents, all day and night.
With every ink squirt, a comic relief,
Ink spills laughter, never any grief.

Join the riddle, let's dive in deep,
To a realm where silly fish dreams leap.
Underwater gigs, with a twist and a song,
In the fun-loving tide, we all belong!

Oceanic Overture of Belonging

Beneath the waves, a party ignites,
Where fish wear hats and dance in tights.
With barnacles pulling off the best pranks,
They host a shindig, down in the tanks.

A crab in a bowtie clinks a beer,
With seahorses lining up to cheer.
Each splash a giggle, each frolic a tease,
Underwater antics that aim to please.

Manatees mingle, so sweetly they sway,
While jellyfish glow in their own ballet.
With currents flowing, laughter's the thing,
The ocean's hum is a joyous ring.

So come dive in, where the fun won't stop,
In this aquatic world, we laugh and plop.
The waves are our canvas, the sea our friend,
Whimsical moments that never quite end!

Tranquil Waves' Hymn

In the sea, the fish do dance,
Chasing bubbles, what a chance!
A dolphin laughs, it wiggles and twirls,
While starfish play with pearls.

Octopus making silly faces,
In all the funniest places.
They giggle from coral to reef,
Sharing laughs, beyond belief!

A crab does a jig, with sideways flair,
While seaweed waves its crazy hair.
The puffer fish puffs with pride,
As clownfish follow, full of stride.

In underwater fun so bright,
Creatures gather with sheer delight.
With quirky songs that bubble up,
In this joyful, splashy cup!

Elysium of the Ocean Realm

In the depths where sea turtles glide,
A narwhal sings with a quirky side.
His tusk a horn, a wacky sight,
He parades through bubbles, what a delight!

Jellyfish jive in a wiggly line,
With colors that shimmer and simply shine.
A fish tells jokes to a passing ray,
Making waves in a dazzling display!

Seahorses twirl, what a fancy show,
As playful fins go to and fro.
Together they laugh, they spin, they swoosh,
While crabs crack up in a funny hush.

In this realm where joy is grand,
They dance and whirl, a merry band.
With echoes of laughter in the blue,
The ocean smiles in every hue!

Enigma of the Blue Depths

In shadows deep where legends dwell,
A fish with glasses has tales to tell.
He reads a book with great delight,
While a buddy fish giggles at his sight!

Deep in the mystery, so much to see,
A squid draws pictures as happy as could be.
His ink spills laughter in the dark,
A masterpiece, a marine spark!

With bubbles floating, a soft parade,
A sea cucumber joins the charade.
Wobbling sideways, it joins the fun,
In this underwater world, they're never done!

The blue depths hold a quirky charm,
Where every creature can raise their arm.
With wriggly giggles that echo wide,
Underwater antics they won't hide!

Ocean's Heartfelt Aria

In the sea's heart, a tune begins,
With notes of laughter and playful spins.
A whale performs with a wiggly flip,
As dolphins cheer, they dance and slip!

A sea lion joins with a hearty bark,
Clapping fins and making his mark.
With every wave, the music swells,
Bubbles burst like happy bells!

The fish form choirs, all scales align,
Singing sweetly, their voices entwine.
Each note a splash, a joyful sound,
Where ocean humor can be found.

In this concert of waves and blue,
Life's rhythm dances, fresh and new.
With heartful tunes that sail along,
In the ocean's embrace, they all belong!

The Deep's Timeless Tune

In the blue where bubbles bloom,
Whales hum tunes that shake the room.
A silly sound, a bubble fart,
Echoes through the ocean's heart.

Jellyfish dance to the beat,
Octopuses tap their feet.
A disco down in salty brine,
Where every fin has perfect rhyme.

Fish swim by in gossip groups,
Sharing tales of whale-sized whoops.
As seahorses spin and twirl,
Underwater, they dance and swirl.

So if you hear a playful croon,
Remember it's an ocean tune.
Join the party, make a splash,
In the depths where sea life dashes.

Resonance of the Ocean's Giants

In the depths, the laughter rolls,
Giant singers with big goals.
Harmonies that twist and sway,
Turning work to whale-sized play.

Bubbles bounce like silly jokes,
Flippers flap and giggles poke.
Each note drips with ocean's glee,
Even sharks can't help but see.

Turtles bop with clumsy grace,
Finding rhythm in the race.
While dolphins leap in joyful arcs,
Their giggles echo through the parks.

So, listen close to every sound,
In this world where fun is found.
With wiggling tails, they sing and play,
In the deep, they seize the day!

Calligraphy in the Currents

With swirling waves, a script unfolds,
A tale of creatures brave and bold.
Whales write stories with their calls,
In curvy lines that dance and sprawl.

Seashells giggle in the sand,
As fish read with wide-eyed bands.
The flippered authors, such a sight,
Crafting verses day and night.

Giant pens made from seaweed stalks,
Draw on currents like crazy clocks.
A playful art beneath the waves,
Where every splash is what it craves.

So bring your ears, your laughs, your cheer,
Join in the fun, for tunes are near.
With every script, a giggle grows,
In the deep, creativity flows.

Notes from Beneath the Surface

Beneath the waves, a band convenes,
With quirky sounds and silly scenes.
Clams tap drums, and fish strum strings,
Creating chaos, joy it brings.

A sea cucumber plays the flute,
While starfish dance in goofy boots.
The clownfish chuckle, shake and sway,
As bubbles pop in great dismay.

A whale sneezes, what a blast!
The echo travels wide and fast.
The sea critters break out in cheer,
For every note they hold so dear.

So listen close; it's quite the show,
Where laughter and silliness flow.
In watery groves, they sing along,
Crafting joy in a splashy song.

Voices of the Deep

Beneath the waves, they start to hum,
Big blubbery buddies, having such fun.
With voices loud, they go off-key,
Their underwater concert's a sight to see.

They swish and splash with a playful dance,
Look out, swimmin' fish, you don't stand a chance!
Giggles arise from the coral homes,
As whales tell tales of their oceanic tomes.

Bubbles are rising, they're all in glee,
Who knew that whales had such melody?
With a flip and a flop, they end the show,
Leaving the sea with a jazzy flow!

So if you're diving, just lend an ear,
To the quirky tunes of the ocean's cheer.
With laughter and bubbles, it's sure to bring,
A smile to your heart, oh what joy they sing!

Ballad of the Blue Giants

In the deep blue sea, where giants reside,
They gossip and jest, no place to hide.
With belly laughs echoing far and wide,
The ocean's their stage, and they've got pride.

One whale tells a joke, the others all bubble,
With waves of laughter, they burst through the rubble.
Knock-knock jokes and whale puns galore,
It's a comedy night, who could ask for more?

They flip and they splash, making quite the scene,
Fins waggling about, they're a silly marine.
What's the best part of being so big?
Napping all day—oh what a gig!

So borrow some joy from these gentle giants,
And dive into laughter, life's great defiance.
Join in their fun, let your worries float,
With friends in the deep, what a life to gloat!

A Symphony of Ocean Migrations

Around the globe, in chorus they roam,
Each year a grand tour, away from their home.
Tails flinging tales as they swim in a line,
Their yearly reunion is simply divine!

With tunes that echo through water so clear,
The laughter and chatter is a delightful cheer.
"Shall we take a detour?" one grumpy one cries,
And off they go chasing all the blue skies.

They twirl and they whirl with each jump and dive,
In goofy formations, they feel so alive!
With krill on the menu, they party all night,
In the light of the moon, everything feels right.

Migration's a blast, oh what a delight,
With friends by their side, they'll dance 'til it's light.
So cheer for the whales as they frolic and sing,
In the symphony deep, joy's the real king!

Tides of Melancholy

A whale in the deep had a mopey old tune,
He sighed through the waves while watching the moon.
"I lost my favorite jellyfish pal,"
He lamented to fishes in the coral gal.

But just as he drifted in sorrowful thought,
A dolphin darted by, "Hey, give it a shot!
Let's throw a big party; you'll feel better soon!"
And suddenly laughter burst forth like a balloon.

With bubbles and giggles, they raised up the tide,
Melancholy waves turned to joy they can't hide.
So when you feel down with your heart all a-frown,
Just call up your pals, turn that sadness around!

From gloom to a giggle, it's a flip of a switch,
Together in laughter, life gets rich.
With every new wave that crashes the shore,
There's humor to find, so let's laugh evermore!

Enveloping Waves of Song

In the ocean blue, a whale does croon,
Gargling like a baby, waking high noon.
Fish swim by, holding their fins to their ears,
As if they could actually hear, through all the cheers.

With bubbles and giggles, it starts to dance,
Splashing around, giving fish quite a chance.
A sardine orchestra joins in delight,
While sea cucumbers waltz through the night.

When whales gather, it's quite the parade,
Their jiggly tails make quite a charade.
Every splash comes with laughter and fun,
The ocean's a stage, and all are a ton!

So listen up close, there's a message to share,
Join the singing whales—who wouldn't dare?
For in every note, there's a giggle or two,
In the grand salty ball, where the laughter is true.

Echoes of the Majestic Ocean

Whales wail like they just lost their socks,
While dolphins giggle in ray-bouncing flocks.
The octopus claps, one hand on each tentacle,
Singing along in a jig that's so radical.

Under the waves, they create quite the scene,
With menacing grins, not a moment is mean.
The sea turtles bob, matching the beat,
As crabs do the cha-cha with wiggly feet.

The seaweed sways, quite enamored and free,
Rocking to rhythms with glee and esprit.
The squids draw the charts, maps of the fun,
Every loop and swirl, so lively, well done!

Echoes for days, oh how they will sing,
In the laughter-filled waters, joy is the king.
A festival of sounds, a splash-tastic spree,
In the depths of the ocean, what a sight to see!

Beauty in the Deep's Lament

Swimming along, a whale's groan does drift,
It sounds like it's stuck in an oceanic rift.
The seaweed waves back, shaking its head,
'Hey big fella, stop whining, go ahead!'

With a flip and a flop, it tries out a tune,
Like singing a salad while stuck in the moon.
The coral chorus joins in with a cheer,
As angels of the deep say 'Loud and clear!'

Grouchy old shells crack open with frown,
While jellyfish swim by in their bright little gown.
They giggle and glide, finding joy in the strife,
Encouraging the whale to just 'chill out' in life!

For a laugh echoes true, beneath waves and foam,
In the depth where the funny ensure they're at home.
So sing on dear whale, let that song be your groove,
In the vast underwater, just find your move!

Guiding Light of Melodic Tides

Beneath the moon's gaze, the whale starts to hum,
The gulls join in, making quite the fun strum.
With swoops and dives, they sail through the gloom,
Creating a party made just for the bloom.

The flick of a tail sends fish skirts a-twirl,
While sea stars applaud, giving the twine a whirl.
There's mischief in the salt, a jazzy affair,
As fish quip, 'Let's dance, if you dare!'

From depths to the surface, the sounds resonate,
With laughter like bubbles, let's celebrate!
Crippled old crabs hop about, filled with cheer,
While mermaids join round—no hiding, my dear!

So let your heart float on the rhythm of tides,
Join the joyous ballet where laughter abides.
In this oceanic realm where fun knows no bounds,
The light of our melody is joy unconfounds!

Beneath Stars and Waves

Under shimmering stars, they dance,
Big blubbery bodies, a wobbly prance.
With flips and splashes, they start the show,
While dolphins chuckle, 'Oh, look at that blow!'

Bubbles rise up in a sparkling spree,
Fish rolling their eyes, 'What a sight to see!'
A whale in a tuxedo, wearing a grin,
Says, 'Dress code's formal, so let's all jump in!'

Tune of the ocean, a funny refrain,
As sea turtles giggle, ignoring the grain.
Crabs pinch each other in laughter so loud,
While plankton are partying, feeling quite proud.

In this watery world, laughter flows free,
With waves tickling sides of the fish and the sea.
So next time you're gazing at the starry bay,
Remember these antics beneath the big sway.

Calligraphy of the Ocean's Voice

Ink of the sea, it scribbles and swirls,
Inking the tides with their whimsical whirls.
A brush of the waves, oh so delightfully fun,
As they giggle and swirl beneath the bright sun.

Whispers of laughter in salt-laden air,
The fish roll their fins, as if unaware.
With squishy sea cucumbers trying to write,
'No one's doing calligraphy quite like tonight!'

Octopi scribble with arms all askew,
The paper's a kelp, and deep blue's the hue.
They doodle their dreams, with squawks and with strokes,
While seagulls add punchlines to oceanic jokes.

So under the sky, where the sea meets the quill,
Creatures compose as they giggle and thrill.
A tale in the tides, where ink and humor mix,
In this underwater world, the fun never quits.

Song of the Silent Depths

Deep below where the sunlight fades,
Creatures gather for music parades.
A grumpy old clam scowls at the band,
While snails in bow ties create quite the stand.

The jellyfish bounce to the beat that they make,
With a rhythm so funky, it leaves quite a wake.
Anglers flick lights like disco balls bright,
Sardines spin out, 'Now that's out of sight!'

A whale joins in with a deep, belly laugh,
Singing low notes that cause fish to gasp.
'This is a concert to remember for days,
Trust me,' says starfish, 'I've got tons of ways!'

So if you should dive where the silence is deep,
You'll find that the sea offers laughter to keep.
Join in the chorus, let giggles abound,
In this whimsical world where joy can be found.

Resonate with Ocean's Whisper

Soft whispers tickle through waters so blue,
As fish gather round with a sparkly crew.
A crab with a hat gives the opening cheer,
'Stay tuned for the gossip you'll want to hear!'

The dolphins are leaping, bubbles burst wide,
With jokes about seagulls who think they are pride.
'They strut on the beach with their flappy old wings,'
'But look at our flips, we put on real blings!'

The anemones sway to the sound of the tide,
While sea urchins chuckle with pincers applied.
In this sea of giggles, everyone sings,
Where even the starfish can paint with their fins.

So swim down below to this symphony sweet,
Join the laughter and feel that good beat.
The ocean's a place where joy is the norm,
Where every little laugh is a buoyant charm.

Echoes of the Forgotten Deep

In the depths where the bubbles play,
Flippers dance in a silly ballet.
Seaweed wiggles with laughter and cheer,
While fish joke about the clownfish's rear.

Jellyfish bounce like they're at a dance,
Swaying and swirling in a trance.
An octopus says, 'I've lost my sock!'
Did he wear it as a fancy frock?

Crabs side-step in a pinching parade,
Making the waves, their very own shade.
A turtle spins tales of his past,
Saying, "I'm slow, but my stories last!"

So beneath the waves, where giggles abound,
The deep ocean's humor is wonderfully found.
A world where the critters can't help but chortle,
In this hidden realm, life's a big portal.

The Enchantress of the Ocean

With a flip of her tail and a wink of her eye,
She charms the fish with a bubble-filled sigh.
A mermaid sings from her rock by the shore,
But the dolphins complain, "We've heard this before!"

She sprinkles her magic with glitter and glee,
Turning sea cucumbers into fine jewelry.
The sea stars giggle, trying to show,
Her voice is the brightest in the ocean's glow.

A crab joins in, playing castanet,
While sea urchins tap, not missing a set.
"Don't be so salty!" the seashells shriek loud,
As they gather around her, forming a crowd.

So dance with the waves, let the rhythm ignite,
In the ball of the ocean, where laughter takes flight.
With each swish and flick, the depth sings a tune,
Funny fish frolic 'neath the bright shining moon.

Anthem of the Abyssal Choir

In the depths where the funny fish croon,
An octopus tries to hum a cartoon.
Clams clap their shells, keeping the beat,
While seahorses tap dance on their tiny feet.

A whale's thick bass makes the water shake,
As shrimps sing high notes, for goodness' sake!
A grouper quips, "I'd like to join in,"
But all he does is produce a loud win.

As the sea cucumbers join the fun,
Their moves are so slow, they're almost done!
Eels slither like ribbons in the choir,
All singing praises, fueled by desire.

With bubbles as notes and kelp strands as ties,
The deep ocean's laughter reaches the skies.
A coral reef sways, keeping up with the jam,
Laughing all the way, "This is quite the slam!"

Lament of the Ocean Spirits

In the moonlight, the spirits do sigh,
Wishing for snacks as they swim by.
"Seaweed, again?" one says with a pout,
"Can't we order something better, no doubt?"

But krill dance around, making quite the fuss,
Saying, "You're full of it, you husky muss!"
With a flick of their tails and a giggle or two,
They send out a warning, "No food for you!"

The merfolk lament their old love tales,
While sharks glide by wearing glassy scales.
"Who's got time for sadness and sorrow?"
With a chortle and splash, they sing of tomorrow.

The spirits laugh out loud at their blunders,
In the swirling depths where joy never sunders.
Their laughter echoes, a harmonious spree,
In the heart of the ocean, so wild and free!

Melodies in the Ocean's Veil

Bubbles pop like party tunes,
As fins perform a silly dance.
Echoes bounce from June to June,
Whales laughing in a watery trance.

They harmonize with fishy friends,
A choir of gurgles and snickers.
With flips and flops the fun never ends,
Splashes sparking like glittering stickers.

Each note a wave in a playful sea,
Where barnacles join with their own beat.
The dolphins giggle, oh what glee,
As sea turtles sway to the funky heat.

So join the party beneath the blue,
Dance on the tides, give a cheer!
The ocean's laughter is waiting for you,
Join the whales' antics, let's all steer!

Calls of the Marine Giants

Oh, the big ones sing with glee,
Mouths agape in joyful tune.
Bubbling out their melody,
Underneath the fishing moon.

They whale out jokes that cause a splash,
Blubbering laughter, the sea's delight.
The fish all gather, hoping for a dash,
Of tales more fishy than bite!

With every swoop, they throw a jest,
Splashing water with floppy fins.
The ocean's calm can turn to a fest,
With whale-sized humor, nobody sins.

From the smallest shrimp to the great blue,
All gather 'round for a matinee.
Giggles abound, the joy is true,
In the underwater cabaret!

Whalesong Reverie

Fins flick like they're crafting a poem,
Waves carry giggles on their crest.
They frolic, swirl, and call it home,
A symphony of laughter, the very best!

With a whoop and a splash, they dive so deep,
Creating ripples of joy that flow.
It's a concert where fish and whales leap,
As the shy octopus sings 'hello!'

Their tunes are silly, each one a laugh,
Bubbling up through the great blue maze.
They break through the surface like a goofy graph,
Cheering on the sun with rhythmic praise!

In the depths of the ocean, you'll find a show,
Where every wave gives a hearty cheer!
Join the whale songs, let your laughter flow,
For in this reverie, there's nothing to fear!

Beneath the Moonlit Sea

Under the glow of a silver light,
The whales begin their nightly spree.
Every croak and chirp feels just right,
As they bellow out rhymes with glee.

Flipping through waves, a tail slaps loud,
The fish giggle, skittering near.
A splash, a laugh, from the jovial crowd,
As seaweed wiggles, oh dear, oh dear!

In the moon's embrace, they dance with flair,
Their songs echo through the deep blue night.
Even plankton join the fun whirling there,
In a swirling party, all taking flight.

So if you listen, you might just hear,
The symphony of joy far and wide.
Join the whales in their ocean cheer,
In the laughter of tides, let your heart glide!

The Ocean's Heartbeat

In the sea where fish do dance,
Whales sing tunes that make them prance.
Splashing waves with a giggle and grin,
Underwater concerts start to begin.

Bubbles burst with a bubbly cheer,
Every note tickles a finny ear.
Clownfish chuckle in a rhythm divine,
While sea turtles groove, feeling simply fine.

Octopus joins with arms all a-sway,
Swaying to rhythms in a playful display.
A dolphin pirouettes and flips so bold,
This ocean party never gets old.

Oh, the mermaids clap to the beat,
Tails wiggling, making life sweet.
With laughter echoing through the spray,
Underwater fun is here to stay.

Liquid Lyrics of the Deep

In the depths where shadows play,
Songs of the sea keep boredom at bay.
Fishy ballads that twist and twine,
Make even the grumpiest angler smile and shine.

Starfish tap dance on coral tops,
Seahorses whirling in bubbly hops.
The jellyfish glows in a quirky trance,
As seaweed sways, they all start to prance.

Anemones sway, their arms in a fuss,
While clams start to hum without any fuss.
The ocean's a stage for a comical show,
With every splash, they steal the flow.

So if you dive where the sea life sings,
You'll find the laughter that the deep sea brings.
Fins and flippers shake with delight,
In this underwater fancy, everything feels right.

Chords of the Celestial Sea

The whales might boast a vocal range,
But octopuses play keys that are strange.
Tuning their tentacles, on coral they press,
Creating a symphony that's bound to impress.

With bubbles and splashes, the octaves rise,
Even seagulls can't help but harmonize.
The fish form a choir, they all gather near,
As starfish join in, lending a fin to the cheer.

Sardines swirl in a synchronized whirl,
While crustaceans dance, out of their shell they twirl.
The ocean's heart beats in sync with the joy,
Every shell and scale plays a role, oh boy!

When night falls, they light up the sea,
As bioluminescent bands set them free.
Giggling and glowing, a sight to behold,
Under the moon, magic stories are told.

Harmonies of the Abyssal Realm

In the abyss where laughter hides,
Creatures play where the darkness collides.
A clownfish jigs in a silly parade,
While a flatfish joins, too shy to invade.

An iron whale yodels, quite out of tune,
Echoing dreams beneath the pale moon.
Squids take the stage, their humor a blast,
With wiggly dance moves unsurpassed.

The anglerfish giggles, showing a grin,
His bait's just a joke, let the mischief begin!
As starry rays flicker with laughter so bright,
Each note of the ocean sparks pure delight.

In this kingdom of joy, every creature sings,
With harmonies that dance on invisible wings.
So dive under waves where fun is the theme,
In the deep's playful world, life's a dream.

Voices of the Blue

In the depths where the seaweed sways,
A fish sings goofy, in bright, silly ways.
Crabs clap along, a zany parade,
As dolphins dance, not a moment to fade.

Whales whisper jokes in echoing tones,
While lobsters giggle, rolling in stones.
With splashes and tunes, they frolic and play,
Creating a ruckus, all night and all day.

A finned choir laughs, oh what a sight!
Telling tales of the ocean, sparkling and bright.
With sea cucumbers joining the fun,
Their antics last long till the day is done.

So listen, dear friend, to the joyful sound,
Where laughter and bubbles always abound.
In the great blue, the chorus is king,
And all kinds of creatures joyfully sing.

Lullabies of the Leviathan

Underneath the waves, gentle giants glide,
Singing sweet tunes with the current as their guide.
Tiny fish dance, caught in the delight,
As the lullabies drift in the soft, moonlit night.

With every great note, the ocean sways,
Turtles nod off in a sleepy malaise.
While octopuses juggle, with eight arms in tow,
The serenade's magic puts on quite a show.

Stars above twinkle, in rhythm they sway,
While squids paint the sea with their colorful play.
As the bubbles rise up, like dreams in the air,
They hum soft lullabies to the sea's cozy lair.

So rest little critters, the sun will return,
With tales of the ocean, for each one to learn.
In the heart of the abyss, where together they dream,
Lullabies swirl, a harmonious theme.

Harmonics of the Abyss

Deep in the ocean, where shadows do twirl,
A sardine concert sets the waves in a whirl.
Clownfish giggling, with bubbles they blow,
While plankton hold hands, putting on a show.

Echos resounding, what a comical tune!
Sea turtles join in, like they're over the moon.
A chorus of jellyfish swaying with grace,
Floating around like they're in a race.

With hiccups and bubbles, the whale takes a breath,
Telling old tales, playing tricks with a jest.
As fish roll on laughing, the sea comes alive,
With harmonics of joy that help all survive.

So remember, dear friend, this oceanic glee,
Where humor and music flow endlessly free.
A underwater stage, where laughter can thrive,
And the rhythms of life keep the magic alive.

Sonorous Secrets of the Sea

In the sea's wide expanse, the secrets all play,
As fish share their gossip in frolicsome way.
A whale's hearty chuckle shakes sand on the floor,
While mermaids roll dice and shout, "Want some more?"

Sea horses gossip, their tails intertwined,
With tales of old shipwrecks, and treasures they find.
Shrimp in tuxedos, how dapper they look,
Officiating weddings by the old forest nook.

With a splash and a swish, they dance through the dark,
While big fish on trumpets create quite the spark.
Octopuses jive, with moves that astound,
As secrets unfold in the depths all around.

So dive into laughter, let the currents be fun,
Each splash tells a story, each wave is a pun.
In the depths of the ocean, where whimsy is free,
The sonorous secrets make merry, you see.

Deep Calls to Deep

In the depths, they hum and dance,
Making waves with their odd romance.
With blubbery tales and goofy grins,
They frolic and flaunt like they're in spins.

A splash here, a splash there, it's all in jest,
Underwater parties, they think they're the best.
With bubbles that tickle and laughter so bold,
These jesters of the sea, a sight to behold!

Moby in overalls, Finny in a hat,
Playing hide and seek with a curious cat.
They race with the current, they leap with delight,
Making sure to cause a ruckus each night.

So next time you sail where the wild waters creep,
Listen close for the laughter from deep in the deep.
You might find a whale or two, full of cheer,
Sharing secrets and giggles for all who are near.

The Ocean's Whispered Wishes

The seagulls squawk in a gossiping tone,
While fish flirt and wiggle, each on their own.
Whales do the cha-cha with style and flair,
In a ballet of bubbles, how can we stare?

From coral reefs dressed in costumes so bright,
To the blushing shrimp who take off in flight.
Octopuses juggling their seven fine hats,
While the sea turtles groove, imagining chats.

"Hey, splash me some brine!" the clam calls out loud,
As dolphins dive deep, feeling oh-so-proud.
With tides that keep time like a grand concert band,
The ocean's a stage with a whimsical hand.

So next time you wonder what's down in the blue,
Hear the chuckles and giggles, they're waiting for you.
For beneath the soft waves, the mischief runs deep,
In this underwater circus, secrets we'll keep.

Tidal Melancholy

The waves crash softly, but there's a tale,
Of a whale who thought he could never set sail.
With a frown on his face, he puffed and he sighed,
"I just want to dance with the fish by my side!"

Bubbles of sorrow from his blowhole burst,
As schools of sardines danced, and he felt worse.
But a dolphin swam by with a wink and a grin,
"Join in our splashes, here, let's begin!"

With a flick and a flop, they twirled through the tide,
Our friend found the rhythm he couldn't abide.
With laughter quite hearty, and moments to save,
The whale turned his blues into splashes and waves.

In the briny deep, where the sun likes to peek,
Sometimes melancholy wears a funny cheek.
For all of us know, it's a dance, not a race,
And joy can be found even in a sad face.

Singing with the Sea

Voices arise from the ocean's grand stage,
As crabs hold their claps in a magical rage.
The whales sing ballads, that echo so sweet,
While sea stars play tambourines with their feet.

"Let's start a party!" the clownfish implores,
Dancing in circles, while opening doors.
With seaweed confetti and laughter like foam,
This underwater choir calls all fish home.

The jellyfish flash with a light-up display,
As conch shells take turns announcing the play.
"Come one, come all, to this festive delight!
We'll waltz with the waves until the morning light!"

So sing with the sea, let your worries depart,
For laughter and joy are the song from the heart.
With frolicsome friends in the ocean so free,
Come join in the rhythm of swimming with glee!

Euphony Under the Swell.

A fish with a kazoo, oh what a sight,
Blowing bubbles, trying with all its might.
The octopus strummed on a jellyfish drum,
Under the sea, they made quite the hum.

The clam joined in, with a clam-shell clap,
While dolphins danced in a synchronized tap.
With laughter they filled the ocean so wide,
A bubbly orchestra, a tidal delight!

The seaweed swayed, a green-tinted dress,
As starfish twinkled in perfect finesse.
They formed a parade down the coral lane,
Reminding us all of the joy in the rain.

In the depths of the blue, where silliness reigns,
Waves carry music that tickles the brains.
So join in the fun, let your worries float,
For life's just a concert, and we're all the note!

Echoes in the Deep

There's a trumpet-blowing fish, oh what a prank,
Trying to sound like an old rusty tank.
The whale took a breath, then let out a laugh,
It echoed so loud, made the seafoam splash!

A lobster in shades was tap dancing too,
Grabbing attention, like a rock star debut.
With crabs in tailcoats and fins in a whirl,
The seabed rumbled, what a fishy swirl!

Sharks joined the fun, sporting top hats so neat,
They shuffled along, with their own funky beat.
While the deep-sea angler lit up the show,
With a glow that made disco seem rather low!

Bubbles floated by, forming laughter-filled trails,
As sea cucumbers narrate the tales.
In the wavy rhythm, where giggles ignite,
The deep is a circus, what a splendid sight!

Melodies Beneath the Waves

With a banjo-strumming porpoise, the fun awaits,
Playing tunes for the fish in their colorful states.
The turtle chimed in with a lopsided grin,
As jellyfish twirled, oh what a din!

In the kelp forest, a sea turtle croons,
To the beat of the waves and the light of the moons.
While clownfish giggle in their vibrant parade,
Creating a ruckus that never will fade.

A narwhal's high note pierced through the blue,
It made the whole ocean join in with a woo!
While seaweed swayed, a crowd full of cheer,
The underwater party became quite the sphere!

With laughs and with songs, they banished all strife,
Together they crafted a buoyant sea life.
So whenever you're down, just look to the tide,
For laughter and melodies forever reside!

Serenade of the Sea

A crab with a fiddle, oh what a delight,
Saw his friend the sea urchin do a jig just right.
With fins all a-flap, fish formed a line,
Serenading the waves with rhythm divine.

The playfulness echoed, from reef far and wide,
Seahorses twirled, with tails open wide.
Anemones clapped, while snails took a bow,
In the realm of the sea, let's have fun, oh wow!

Come join in the laughter, it's a shell of a time,
As eels spin around, in a dance quite sublime.
The briny breeze carried tunes to the shore,
Where creatures of joy sang forevermore!

So let your heart bubble with laughter and cheer,
In the depths and the swells, let your spirit steer.
For each tide brings a song, a playful refrain,
Floating through currents like love in the rain!

Whispered Dreams of the Sea

In the depths where fish do giggle,
A whale hums tunes, a massive riddle.
Starfish dance on ocean floors,
While seaweed sways like merry scores.

Crabs wear hats and sing a tune,
They prance around, but not too soon.
A dolphin flips, a splashy cheer,
While turtles plot their next career.

Bubbles rise like playful sprites,
Tickling fish in silly flights.
The octopus makes quite the scene,
Dressed in colors, oh so keen!

Underwater laughter fills the blue,
A symphony of joy anew.
As waves of humor gently flow,
In the sea's embrace, we all can grow.

Ocean's Heartfelt Harmony

In the ocean's chuckle, crabs align,
Playing cards while sipping brine.
A narwhal jokes with a wink of light,
His tusk a sword in the playful fight.

Fish in bow ties swirl and twirl,
As jellyfish swirl in a gooey hurl.
Seahorses prance like fancy men,
Donning shades, they party again!

Stars above envy the show,
As bubbles pop, rhythms flowed.
Gulls caw jokes, diving for a laugh,
While clownfish watch from their signed path.

The sea's a stage, with tales to spill,
Where laughter echoes, and time stands still.
To the ocean's pulse, we dance along,
In the harmony of every song.

Embrace of the Oceanic Echo

With a swish and a wiggle, a whale does tease,
As otters tumble with utter ease.
The dolphins giggle, a splash brigade,
In an ocean of jokes, we're never afraid.

Clownfish wave from coral thrones,
While sea cucumbers hum soft tones.
A kraken in a tutu takes center stage,
Shaking its tentacles, a true sea sage!

Flipping backwards, the dolphins wink,
As turtles join in, they think and think.
A bubble parade with shrimp on the go,
Making waves in the undertow!

From sea to sea, let laughter sail,
In a world where humor shall prevail.
In the embrace of the ocean's fun,
Every creature shines, and we are all one.

Journey of the Resonant Beasts

A journey starts with a belly flop,
As whales launch forth with a plop and a pop.
Sea anemones giggle, catching the breeze,
While starfish collaborate with mischievous tease.

On bubbles, the lobsters twist and shout,
In underwater parties, there's never a doubt.
Each wave carries tales of laughter and pride,
As crabs take selfies, cramming inside.

An octopus wearing a polka dot hat,
Swings to the rhythm, looking quite sprat.
A finned disco boat with briny beats,
Where even sea urchins dance on their feet!

Through colorful reefs and kelp on a swing,
The ocean's voice is a humorous thing.
With every swish and a splashy blare,
The journey is filled with joy to share.

www.ingramcontent.com/pod-product-compliance
Lightning Source LLC
Chambersburg PA
CBHW062110280426
43661CB00086B/408